Sherlock Holmes and the case of Dr Freud

MICHAEL SHEPHERD

M.A., D.M., F.R.C.P., F.R.C.PSYCH., D.P.M.

TAVISTOCK PUBLICATIONS
London and New York

First published in 1985 by
Tavistock Publications Ltd
11 New Fetter Lane, London EC4P 4EE

Published in the USA by
Tavistock Publications
in association with Methuen, Inc.
733 Third Avenue, New York, NY 10017

British Library Cataloguing in Publication Data

Shepherd, Michael, *1923*–
Sherlock Holmes and the case of Dr. Freud.
1. Freud, Sigmund   2. Doyle, *Sir* Arthur Conan
I. Title
150.19′52   BF173.F85

ISBN 0-422-79990-4

Library of Congress Cataloging in Publication Data

Shepherd, Michael, 1923–
Sherlock Holmes and the case of Dr Freud.
1. Doyle, Arthur Conan, Sir, 1859–1930 – Characters –
Sherlock Holmes. 2. Holmes, Sherlock (Fictitious
character) 3. Freud, Sigmund, 1856–1939. 4. Psychoanalysis and literature. 5. Detective and mystery
stories, English–History and criticism. I. Title.
PR4624.S44   1985   823′.8   85-2795
ISBN 0-422-79990-4

Designed by Carlos Sapochnik
Photoset by Rowland Phototypesetting Ltd
Bury St Edmunds, Suffolk
Printed in Great Britain at
the University Printing House, Cambridge

This essay is based on the
1984 Squibb History of Psychiatry lecture,
which was delivered at the
Institute of Psychiatry, London,
in June 1984.

The author and publishers would like to thank the
following for permission to reproduce copyright
material: Dr D. F. Musto for the frontispiece 'Sherlock
Holmes and Sigmund Freud' from his article 'A Study
in Cocaine' (see Note 18); Deborah Rogers Ltd and
Harvard University Press for the illustrations on p. 14
and p. 15 and the extract on p. 16 from Richard
Wollheim (see Note 29); and the BBC Hulton Picture
Library for the illustration on p. 18.

The death of Professor Moriarty.

Freud and Holmes

IT HAS BECOME a truism to maintain that most physicians, and all psychiatrists, can benefit professionally from some familiarity with the world of fiction. The works of such major artists as Balzac, Dickens, Shakespeare, and Ibsen, and those of many lesser writers, contain a host of characters depicting various morbid states of mind encountered in clinical practice. For this reason they illustrate, and often supersede, most textbooks of abnormal psychology and psychopathology.

But there is more to fiction than the portrayal of character. Writing of the art-form which he did so much to create Balzac observed that the province of the novel is the history of human manners, the nature of man's perception of himself, and the embodiment of ideas. One of these embodied ideas introduces my theme and does so, modestly enough, in the form of a detective story. The story in question is Nicholas Meyer's *The Seven Per Cent Solution*, a best-seller in several languages, winner of the Crime Writer's Golden Dagger Award, and the basis of a successful film.[1] The book purports to be a reprint from the reminiscences of Dr John H. Watson, the trusty friend and companion of the prince of detectives, Mr Sherlock Holmes. In it Watson recounts the true story of what happened after Holmes's disappearance and supposed death near the Reichenbach Falls, following a struggle with the infamous Professor Moriarty.

On his surprising reappearance three years later Holmes claimed originally to have been travelling incognito, using the pseudonym of a Norwegian explorer called Sigerson. According to *The Seven Per Cent Solution* the facts were very different. Sherlock Holmes, it appears, was suffering from a severe mental disorder with delusional ideas concerning the machinations of Professor Moriarty, who was in reality a harmless teacher of mathematics. Tricked by Watson's ruse to provide him with medical care, Holmes travels to Vienna for treatment by a young physician specializing in nervous diseases who cures him by hypnosis and succeeds in identifying the roots of his long-standing malaise. The two men then join in a successful hunt for a local villain who is attempting to precipitate a world war.

Exciting as it is, however, the narrative is less relevant than the identity of the doctor, who is none other than Sigmund Freud. At their first meeting Freud is bowled over by his patient's ability to provide him with an accurate biographical sketch after no more than a brief glance round the consulting-room:

'"Beyond the fact", says Holmes "that you are a brilliant physician who was born in Hungary and studied for a time in Paris, and that some radical theories of yours have alienated the respectable medical community so that you have severed your connections with various hospitals and branches of the medical fraternity – beyond the fact that you have ceased to practise medicine as a result, I can deduce little. You are married, possess a sense of honour, and enjoy playing cards and reading Shakespeare and a Russian author whose name I am unable to pronounce. I can say little besides that which will be of interest to you."

Freud stared at Holmes for a moment in utter shock. Then, suddenly he broke into a smile . . .

"But this is wonderful!" he exclaimed.

"Commonplace", was the reply.'

As the tale unfolds it becomes apparent that the connection between the two men depends on more than a literary device bringing together a fictional detective with personal problems and a well-known psychiatrist. The force of the story would clearly be lost if the protagonists were substituted by, say, Emil Kraepelin and Lord Peter Wimsey. The affinity between the two principal characters becomes increasingly apparent to Dr Watson, as it had to me years earlier when reading Freud's case-histories. The very names of those memorable patients – the Wolf Man, the Rat Man, Anna O, Little Hans – conjure up Sherlockian overtones. Take, for example, the Wolf Man, or Sergei Konstantinovich Pankeyev, to give him his true name. His condition has baffled many other specialists, including Kraepelin, before he undergoes psychoanalysis by Freud who gradually traces the neurosis to its source in the primal scene.[2] In the process the patient is 'cured', the mystery is dispelled, and the truth revealed by a detached individual of superior ability who alone sees what lesser men fail to comprehend, and who draws quite unexpected conclusions from his observations. The whole pattern of presentation recalls G. K. Chesterton's description of the true object of an intelligent detective story – 'not to baffle the reader, but to enlighten him in such a manner that each successive portion of the truth comes as a surprise. In this, as in much nobler types of mystery, the object . . . is not merely to mystify but to illuminate.'

Psychoanalysis has, of course, been compared to detection by several observers, including Freud himself, who defended his activities in the *Introductory Lectures* by asking:

'Suppose you are a detective engaged in the investigation of a murder, do you actually expect to find that the murderer will leave his photograph with name and address on the scene of the crime? Are you not perforce content with slighter and less certain traces of the person you seek?'[3]

Still more to the point is a passage in the Wolf Man's personal recollections, in which he discusses his therapist's choice of literature:

'Once when we happened to speak of Conan Doyle and his creation, Sherlock Holmes, I had thought that Freud would have no use for this type of light reading matter, and was surprised to find that this was not at all the case and that Freud had read this author attentively. The fact that circumstantial evidence is useful in psychoanalysis when reconstructing a childhood history may explain Freud's interest in this type of literature.'[4]

As if to confirm the connection, in one of his letters to Jung on a delicate personal matter Freud refers explicitly to his activities: 'I made it appear as though the most tenuous of clues had enabled me, Sherlock Holmes-like, to guess the situation.'[5]

Here, then, is a curious association. To his admirers Freud tends to be either a nonpareil or a scientific giant comparable to the likes of Kepler, Copernicus, and Darwin. Abram Kardiner's opinion may serve as representative:

'This adventure of self-discovery, recorded in *The Interpretation of Dreams*, has, to my mind, been equalled in human history only a few times. It is an odyssey of far greater intensity than is recorded in the *Confessions* of St Augustine, and much more sincere and modest than those that are contained in the *Confessions of Rousseau*. *The Interpretation of Dreams* is restrained; yet it ranks in intensity with the kind of inner self-encounter and honesty that must have preceded the creation of Kant's *Critique of Pure Reason* and Einstein's general theory of relativity.'[6]

What can such a man have in common with any fictional character, however prominent? In the *Timaeus* Plato remarks that: 'It is impossible that two things be joined without a third. There must be some bond to bring them together.' The nature of that bond is the theme of this essay.

Cocaine

ONE OBVIOUS POINTER to its nature is contained in the title of Meyer's book. *The Seven Per Cent Solution* refers to the drug cocaine, which figured prominently in the careers of both Holmes and Freud. As early as 1887 we know from Dr Watson that his friend had been 'alternating from week to week between cocaine and ambition', and the journey to Vienna was undertaken because of Freud's published work on cocaine.

Several other physicians and pharmacologists have since interested themselves in the nature of Holmes's drug-dependence. Nearly fifty years ago the *Lancet* carried an anonymous article entitled 'Was Sherlock Holmes a Drug Addict?', arguing that when the great detective told Watson that he was injecting himself with cocaine he was pulling the worthy doctor's leg.[7] The nature of the substance was later disputed by Miller, who asserted that the drug in question must have been a belladonna alkaloid because of the moral and physical deterioration associated with the use of cocaine.[8] This view was in turn contested by Grilly,[9] citing no less an authority than Goodman and Gilman's *The Pharmacological Basis of Therapeutics* in which it is stated that 'Sherlock Holmes took advantage of the central effects of cocaine, much to the perturbation of Dr Watson'.[10] Another eminent pharmacologist, Walter Modell, remarks that 'Although habit-forming, cocaine is not tenaciously so, and since it is not physiologically addictive, strong personalities like Freud and Sherlock Holmes had no trouble in controlling the habit.'[11]

The facts were rather different. Sherlock Holmes's creator, Sir Arthur Conan Doyle, carried out a number of experiments with a self-administered drug, but the substance in question was the relatively harmless gelsemium.[12] Freud's experiences with cocaine, on the other hand, were altogether more unfortunate. Ernest Jones's biography provides an outline of events: the early work with and enthusiasm for the 'magical drug'; the under-emphasis on its dangers, culminating in the suicide of a friend whom he persuaded to substitute cocaine for morphine; the failure to appreciate the significance of its properties as a local anaesthetic; and the ultimate disillusionment, without full acceptance of responsibility.[13] Even the hagiographic Jones is compelled to admit that many observers 'must at least have regarded him as a man of reckless judgement'. Others have gone further, seeing in this episode a microcosm of Freud's career, while Thornton has even suggested that the influence of cocaine played a much longer-lasting part in Freud's outlook than has been recognized.[14]

It is the effects of the drug on Sherlock Holmes, however, which are more relevant to our theme, for in 1966 an American psychiatrist, David Musto, first suggested that Holmes was suffering from a delusional illness associated with chronic cocainism which he called *paranoia moriartii*.[15] Musto's paper, which appeared in the *Journal of the American Medical Association*, was followed by letters of rebuttal, some affirming that Holmes was manic-depressive,[16] others that he merely suffered from occupational inertia.[17] In 1968 Musto elaborated on his notion in a paper entitled 'A Study in Cocaine', pointing out that the drug had stimulated the careers of two brilliant investigators, Sigmund Freud and Sherlock Holmes.[18] He suggested that between 1891 and 1894 Holmes had been recuperating under treatment, perhaps in Switzerland, but possibly in 'a pleasant sanatorium in the Viennese suburbs'. This would, of course, eliminate the pseudonymous Sigerson, though not without a reminder that this was the name of the neurologist who translated Charcot into English, shortly after Freud had translated him into German.[19] Musto's suggestion is also, of course, the origin of *The Seven Per Cent Solution*.

Zadig's method

BUT IT IS the enticing speculation which Musto derives from his theory to which I would draw particular attention:

'His ideas and especially his methods must have influenced those to whom he spoke. We are accustomed to the attention Holmes paid to the unusual fact, the unravelling of a complicated problem from the noting of a small slip or characteristic. This style of reasoning may have been the gift of Holmes to those who treated him for his temporarily inefficient mental processes.'

To illustrate Holmes's 'style of reasoning', here is an early sample. The trusty Dr Watson has just arrived unexpectedly at 221B Baker Street, hoping to persuade the great man to accompany him on holiday. Before he can open his mouth Holmes tells him of the purpose of his visit:

'"Knowing you as I do, it's absurdly simple," said he. "Your surgery hours are from 5 to 7, yet at 6 o'clock you walk smiling into my rooms. Therefore you must have a locum in. You are looking well though tired, so the obvious reason is that you are having, or are about to have, a holiday. The clinical thermometer, peeping out of your pocket proclaims that you have been on your rounds today; hence it's pretty evident that your real holiday begins tomorrow. When, under these circumstances, you come hurrying into my rooms – which, by the way, Watson, you haven't visited for nearly three months – with a new Bradshaw and a time-table of excursion bookings bulging out of your coat pocket, then it's more than probable you have come with the idea of suggesting some joint expedition."'

According to Musto, it is the mode of thought underlying passages of this type which constitutes the link that we have been seeking. This consists in the use of a method. And in *The Seven Per Cent Solution* this is acknowledged when Holmes responds to Freud's comment that his professional outlook is akin to medical observation by remarking: 'You have succeeded in taking my methods – observation and inference – and applied them to the inside of a subject's head.'

In the original canon Holmes is too concerned with demonstrating the value of this method to discuss its theoretical implications. Fortunately, we can turn to his real-life prototype for the purpose. Sherlock Holmes was modelled partly on Edgar Allan Poe's C. Auguste Dupin and partly on one of Conan Doyle's teachers, Joseph Bell, the Edinburgh surgeon whose powers of observation and diagnostic acumen were legendary. Conan Doyle made no secret of his debt to Bell, a man with 'sharp, piercing grey eyes, eagle nose, and striking features',[20] who could:

'diagnose people as they came in, before even they had opened their mouths. He would tell them their symptoms, he would give them details of their lives, and he would hardly ever make a mistake. "Gentlemen", he would say to us students standing around, "I am not quite sure whether this man is a cork-cutter or a slater. I observe a slight callus, or hardening on one side of the forefinger, and a little thickening on the outside of his thumb, and that is a sure sign he is either one or the other."[21]

In a letter to his old teacher, Doyle says of Holmes:

'I do not think that his analytical work is in the least an exaggeration of some of the effects which I have seen you produce in the out-patient ward. Round the centre of deduction and inference and observation which I have heard you inculcate I have tried to build up a man who pushed the thing as far as it would go.'[22]

Bell responded modestly to the compliment:

'The only credit I can take to myself in what Holmes says is that appertaining to the circumstances that I always impressed over and over again upon all my scholars – Conan Doyle among them – the vast importance of little distinctions, the endless significance of trifles.'[23]

In his critique of the stories, Bell acknowledged the growing interest by the public in detective fiction, and the narrative skill of the author who had created a 'shrewd, quick-sighted, inquisitive man, half doctor, half virtuoso'. But at the core of the achievement he identified a method:

'There is nothing new under the sun. Voltaire taught us the method of Zadig, and every good teacher of medicine or surgery exemplifies every day in his teaching and practice the method and its results. The precise and intelligent recognition and appreciation of minor differences is the real essential factor in all successful medical diagnosis. Carried into ordinary life, granted the presence of an insatiable curiosity and fairly acute sense, you have Sherlock Holmes as he astonishes his somewhat dense friend Dr Watson; carried out in a specialized training, you have Sherlock Holmes the skilled detective.'[24]

Bell's reference to Zadig compels us to go back to Voltaire's wonderful fable, whose eponymous hero furnishes a detailed description of a horse which he has never seen, giving his reasons as follows:

'In the lanes of this wood, I observed the marks of a horse's shoes, all at equal distances. This must be a horse, said I to myself, that gallops excellently. The dust on the trees in a narrow road that was but 7 feet wide was a little brushed off, at the distance of 3 feet and a half from the middle of the road. The horse, said I, has a tail 3 feet and a half long, which being whisked to the right and the left has swept away the dust. I observed, under the trees that formed an arbour 5 feet in height, that the leaves of the branches were newly fallen; from whence I inferred that the horse had touched them, and that he must therefore be 5 feet high. As to his bit, it must be gold of 23 carats, for he had rubbed its bosses against a stone which I knew to be a touchstone, and which I had tested. In a word, from the marks made by his shoes on flints of another kind, I concluded that he was shod with silver eleven deniers fine.'[25]

Even Holmes could not have done better! It may be remarked, parentheti-cally, that this passage is itself derivative, being based on a translation of a sixteenth-century collection of stories about the travels of the three sons of the king of Serendippo, a book which prompted Horace Walpole to coin the term 'serendipity' in 1745. More than a century later Zadig's method came into its own as the cornerstone of what is sometimes called 'conjectural science'. Zadig is mentioned by name in Georges Cuvier's monumental study of palaeontology and the method receives detailed attention in an influential essay by T. H. Huxley, published in 1881 and entitled 'On the Method of Zadig: Retrospective Prophecy as a Function of Science'.[26] Huxley concludes that:

> 'The rigorous application of Zadig's logic to the results of accurate and long-continued observation has founded all those sciences which have been termed historical or palaetiological, because they are retrospectively pro-phetic and strive towards the reconstruction in human imagination of events which have vanished or ceased to be.'

Huxley is here echoing William Whewell's famous exposition of the logic of induction.[27] Though his primary concern with 'retrospective prophecy' was related to his view of Darwinism as a scientific procedure dealing with unrepeat-able causes which had to be deduced from their consequences, the method of reasoning, as he emphasized, is common to several physical sciences, including archaeology, palaeontology, astronomy, geology, and the semiotics of medicine. And, he might have added, to the scientific study of the humanities in the fields of literature (as stylometrics) and of the history of the visual arts, where scientific connoisseurship dates from the work of the Italian physician, Giovanni Morelli (1816–91).

Morelli

ATTRIBUTION IN PAINTING, as Morelli demonstrated, could only be established by detailed study of the work itself, and in distinguishing the work of a master from that of a copyist he emphasized the necessity of concentrating on what had hitherto been regarded as trivial details. In his own words:

> 'As most men who speak or write have verbal habits and use their favourite words or phrases involuntarily and sometimes even most inappropriately, so almost every painter has his own peculiarities which escape him without his being aware of them. . . . Anyone, therefore, who wants to study a painter closely, must discover these material trifles and attend them with care.'[28]

The successful application of the Morelli method, achieving attribution through retrospective prophecy, has been clearly analysed by modern art critics:

'Morelli's real contribution to the study of art was that he devised a method whereby (according to him) the gap between attribution and work of art could be so effectively bridged that we could talk of its being virtually certain that a particular painting was the work of a particular artist. Morelli's contention was this: every true artist is committed to the repetition of certain characteristic forms or shapes. If we want to determine the authorship of a work of art, we can do so only via recognizing the fundamental forms, the *Grundformen* of the artist to whom it is due. To identify the characteristic forms of an artist, we must go to those parts of the painting where these conventional pressures are likely to be relaxed; even if this means that we shall have to consider what to an educated aesthete of the last century could only have seemed "trifles". We must take seriously the depiction of the hand, the drapery, the landscape, the ball of the thumb, or the lobe of the ear.'[29]

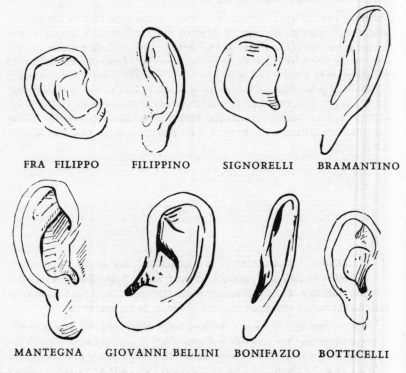

FRA FILIPPO   FILIPPINO   SIGNORELLI   BRAMANTINO

MANTEGNA   GIOVANNI BELLINI   BONIFAZIO   BOTTICELLI

Typical forms of ears, according to Morelli.

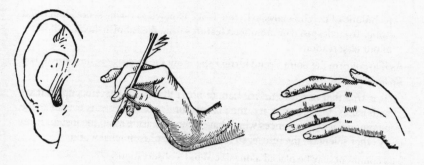

Ears and hands of Botticelli, according to Morelli.

It is not always recalled that Conan Doyle's Uncle Henry was Director of the Dublin Art Gallery and an admirer of Morelli, who in turn referred to him as 'the splendid Mr Doyle'. Whatever the significance of their contacts may have been, the parallels between the teachings of Morelli and Sherlock Holmes are apparent and have been noted by several scholars. The art historian Arturo Castelnuovo has drawn attention to the resemblance between their methods;[30] Edgar Wind refers pointedly to the 'characteristic trifles by which an artist gives himself away, as a criminal might be spotted by a fingerprint';[31] and Carlo Ginzburg brings Holmes and Morelli together, 'each discovering, from clues unnoticed by others, the author in one case of a crime, in the other of a painting'.[32]

Not many physicians, though, might have been expected to be aware of Morelli's work. There was, however, one eminent exception. After his self-confessed 'discovery of art' in 1883 Sigmund Freud became keenly interested in art history and in his essay on 'The Moses of Michelangelo' he made a striking admission:

'Long before I had any opportunity of hearing about psychoanalysis I learnt that a Russian art-connoisseur Ivan Lermolieff had caused a revolution in the art-galleries of Europe by questioning the authorship of many pictures, showing how to distinguish copies from originals with certainty and con-structing hypothetical artists for those works of art whose former authorship has been discredited. He achieved this by insisting that attention should be diverted from the general impression and main features of a picture and by laying stress on the significance of minor details, of things like the drawing of the fingernails, of the lobe of an ear, of halos and such unconsidered trifles which the copyist neglects to imitate and yet which every artist executes in his own characteristic way. I was then greatly interested to learn that the Russian pseudonym concealed the identity of an Italian physician called Morelli, who died in 1891. It seems to me that his method of inquiry is closely related to the technique of psychoanalysis. It, too, is accustomed to divine secret concealed things from despised or unnoticed features from the rubbish-heap, as it were, of our observations.'[33]

As if to confirm the point Freud further spells out the message in the *Introductory Lectures*:

'It is true that psycho-analysis cannot boast that it has never occupied itself with trifles. On the contrary, the material of its observations is usually those commonplace occurrences which have been cast aside as all too insignificant by other sciences, the refuse, so to speak of the phenomenal world.'[3]

His comment may be placed alongside Wind's observation:

'To some of Morelli's critics it has seemed odd "that personality should be found where personal effort is weakest". But on this point modern psychology would certainly support Morelli: our inadvertent little gestures reveal our character more authentically than any formal posture that we may carefully prepare.'[31]

Commenting on the common ground between Morelli and Freud, Wollheim makes the connection directly:

'For Morelli a detail was important, if, first, it is free from conventional pressures and, secondly . . . it has a significance for the artist; just as, in Freudian analysis, a trait must first have acquired a meaning for the person . . . before it can do so for the analyst.'[29]

And Arnold Hauser goes still further:

'Psychoanalysis tries to detect stylistic character from accessories, from unobvious yet revealing details rather than from essentials. Being a kind of psychology of exposure, it follows up clues rather than plain and direct forms of expression and expects the artist to give himself away, more or less as a neurotic patient does, neglecting, however, the fundamental difference, that the meaning of a style is not a puzzle, but a guide. In accord with the spirit of his detective work, Freud was deeply impressed by Morelli's method in art history as an attempt to establish the identity of stylistic trends, above all from those features of a work of art which had least to do with the artist's conscious and deliberate ways of expression. That is to say, the fashion in which a painter has drawn an ear or formed a finger, the character of his handwriting, of which he might not even have been aware, was, Morelli claimed, more revealing than the features by which he meant to express himself most clearly.'[34]

So far, so good. But if Zadig's method of retrospective prophecy helps bridge the gap between our doctor and our fictional detective, it remains to enquire why this particular piece of fiction? To answer this question it becomes necessary to look more closely at the phenomenon rather than at the stories and the character of Mr Sherlock Holmes.

The phenomenon of Sherlock Holmes

Holmes FIRST APPEARED in 1887 in a story published in *Beeton's Christmas Annual* by an unknown young physician, Arthur Conan Doyle (*Illustration 4*). Success was instantaneous and prolonged. The six stories that were originally commissioned eventually extended to sixty. They made Conan Doyle a rich man, enabling him to give up medicine, and in the process the character began to overshadow its creator. As early as 1893, when the *Strand Magazine* announced the impending death of Sherlock Holmes, public reaction was evident: mourning bands were worn in the City and the event was headline news in the foreign press. Holmes's resurrection led to an even greater mass response and many thousands of letters asking for help were addressed to 221B Baker Street. Nor was the interest confined to anglophonic readers. In 1895 an Arabic translation of the early stories was said to have been issued to the Egyptian police force as a textbook. France underwent an outbreak of 'Sherlockitis' inspired by a M. Herlock Sholmès, and a rash of medico-legal studies based on the canon. The Germans coined a new verb, 'sherlockieren' (to deduce or track down), and 'Sherlockismus' was compared with Werthermania. In Spain and Latin America Sherlockholmistos spread rapidly and the Russian, Turkish, and Rumanian versions of the stories were rapturously received; in the Soviet Union they were to be recommended to the Red Army as a model of 'magnificent strength and great culture'.

As early as 1902, furthermore, the *Cambridge Review* carried an open letter to Dr Watson concerning the dates given in *The Hound of the Baskervilles*. This was the forerunner of a huge secondary literature which has included scholarly essays, journals, parodies, plays, and filmscripts. To date Holmes has been the subject of some three hundred films, a ballet, and several books, including eight full-scale biographies. Three bibliographies of Holmesiana have been published, each containing more than six thousand items.

For the most part Conan Doyle was both mystified and irritated by these developments. As early as 1896 he announced that Holmes was 'dead and damned' and that he felt towards him as he would to an overdose of *pâté de foie gras*. The success of Sherlock Holmes, he maintained, overshadowed his more original writings and his major work on spiritualism. None the less, after Doyle's death in 1930 a metempsychosis occurred and the reputation of the character has continued to grow steadily. Except for the Bible, no other writings have been published in as many different languages and editions as the tales of Sherlock Holmes. Visitors to London today who consult their *Michelin Guide* will find the entry for Baker Street beginning: 'The wide thoroughfare was 100 years old when Sherlock Holmes in the 1880s went to live at 221B.' In 1941 *The Times* carried an obituary commenting on the fiftieth year of Holmes's first demise. The British Society of Sherlockians meets regularly to dine at the Law Society

Sir Arthur Conan Doyle.

and discuss the master and his exploits. The Japanese have a society, a magazine, and a pub in Tokyo, the 'Sherlock Holmes', with artificial fog on the ceiling. Other prominent associations perpetuating the legend include the 'Baker Street Irregulars', the 'Speckled Band of Boston', the 'Creeping Men of Cleveland', and 'The Wisteria Lodge Confederates of the Eastern Deep South', all with their individual rituals and apparel, and mostly containing a strong representation of physicians, especially medical historians. Much speculation has been devoted to particular diagnostic issues. What was the nature of Dr Watson's war wound? Did Holmes suffer from Marfan's Syndrome? And, as we have seen, was he dependent on cocaine?

From even these bare facts, then, it is apparent that in less than a hundred years the character of Sherlock Holmes has come to transcend time and space. As recently as July 1984 *The Times* could carry a letter entitled, 'Greatly Exaggerated' by a reader complaining that he was:

'disturbed to read in your columns . . . a reference to "the late Mr Holmes". I trust that since Mr Sherlock Holmes's death has not been confirmed in your obituary columns you will request your excellent Executive Editor not to spread such unjustified rumours of the loss of one of England's greatest men in future.'[35]

As Orson Welles has observed, he is a man who never lived but will never die. He has, in short, left the world of fiction to enter the realms of myth.

Myth and mythod

MYTHOLOGICAL CHARACTERS ARE of central importance to creative writers and can be subdivided into two categories: those which are apocryphal (e.g. Faust, King Arthur, Don Juan), and those which are the products of an individual author's imagination (e.g. Frankenstein, Don Quixote). The capacity to create such characters, furthermore, is often independent of artistic merit, a point made with some authority by the poet, W. H. Auden:

'All characters who are products of the mythopoeic imagination are instan-taneously recognizable by the fact that their existence is not defined by their social and historical context. . . . In consequence, once they have been created, they cease to be their author's characters and become the reader's; he can continue their story for himself. Anna Karenina is not such a character, for the reader cannot imagine her apart from the particular milieu in which Tolstoi places her or the particular history of her life which he records; Sherlock Holmes, on the other hand, is: every reader, according to his fancy, can imagine adventures for him which Conan Doyle forgot, as it were, to tell us. Tolstoi was a very great novelist, Conan Doyle a very minor one, yet it is the minor not the major writer who possesses the mythopoeic gift. The mythopoeic imagination is only accidentally related, it would seem, to the talent for literary expression.'[36]

The phenomenon of Sherlock Holmes becomes comprehensible only if the character is viewed as the representation of a method embedded in a myth. Then it also becomes possible to appreciate the force of a central paradox, namely that the presentation of Zadig's method is a counterfeit, a simulacrum of the real thing, what might be termed neologistically a 'mythod'. As a contemporary physician has remarked, the Sherlockian mode of procedure 'although labelled as deductive and logical, is really intuitive and illogical, but it is so appealingly human that it is enjoyable in contrast to the tedium of a true analytic detective story'.[37] Thus in the example quoted earlier, a moment's reflection makes it apparent that there are several other explanations for Watson's irregular conduct. 'Therefore', 'obvious', 'evident', 'more than probable', says Holmes, but what he describes as 'absurdly simple' might as well have been termed 'simply absurd'. Hugh Kingsmill characterized Sherlock Holmes as an 'inspired imbecile', and Joseph Bell himself referred to the 'cataract of drivel for which Conan Doyle is responsible'. Christopher Isherwood drew the irreverent but inescapable conclusion when he described him as 'one of the truly great comic characters in our literature ... the classic caricature of the Amateur Detective in whose person the whole art of detection is made ridiculous ... [this] is what makes Holmes lovable and immortal'.[38]

Lovable and immortal, perhaps, but more a model of dogmatic assumption than of scientific detection. As one of Doyle's biographers remarks of the Holmes stories: 'It is only deduction if the reader can be made to believe that it is, by suspending his critical faculties.'[39] Within the protective carapace of a myth, however, reality assumes a different meaning. We enter another sphere of logic and it is only in these terms that we can at last approach the case of Dr Freud in its broader historical context.

Psychoanalysis and myth

IN HIS 1908 preface to *The Interpretation of Dreams*, Freud commented sourly on its neglect by the three professional groups for whom it was written, attributing the demand for a second edition principally to what he termed the 'wider circle of educated and curious-minded readers'.[40] This was the circle which was to expand so greatly that in the preface to a subsequent edition Freud admitted candidly that: 'Just as formerly I was unwilling to regard the neglect of my book by readers as evidence of its worthlessness, so I cannot claim that the interest which is now being taken in it is a proof of its excellence.'

With the passage of time the significance of his verdict has become increasingly apparent. Freud himself attached prime importance to his scientific method, to having discovered what James Strachey calls 'the first instrument for the examination of the human mind'.[41] The three groups for whom his work was intended were the clinicians, the scientists, and the philosophers, but after more than three generations it is apparent that for the most part none of these groups has endorsed either his method or its application. The reasons for their refusal to do so are now so well known as to qualify for what Sherlock Holmes would have called the 'commonplace', and call for no more than a brief mention. For the clinicians it is chiefly the therapeutic claims of psychoanalysis which have been eroded, leading to a sharp decline in its prestige, even in the United States where it was most widely incorporated in clinical practice.[42] In his searching and lucid critique of the topic Sir Peter Medawar places particular emphasis on this issue as 'the only independent criterion by which the acceptability of psycho-analytic notions can be judged'.[43] For the biological scientist, he continues, the subject-matter of psychoanalysis is essentially unbiological and is rarely susceptible to experimental examination; and for the philosopher of science it fails to meet the fundamental criteria of refutation. The evidence marshalled by Fisher and Greenberg testifies to the effort invested in attempts to evaluate the theory and practice of psychoanalysis, the difficulties attendant on such an enterprise, and the ambiguity of the findings.[44]

What distinguishes Medawar's negative critique from that of most other scientists, however, is his further insistence that in as much as psychoanalysis merits consideration it does so not as a science but as a form of mythology which 'brings some kind of order into incoherence; it . . . hangs together, makes sense, leaves no loose ends, and is never (but never), at a loss for explanation. In a state of bewilderment it may therefore bring comfort and relief.'[45] Medawar does not mean this as a compliment. As a scientific rationalist he favours Voltaire's view of all myths as fairy stories for savages, in this case forms of science fiction which echo the Romantic syllogism that lies can be myths which may in turn represent forms of truth. As far as it goes, his argument is watertight, challenging the dictionary definition of a myth as a story invented as a veiled explanation of a truth. For Medawar and like-minded critics there is no truth since: 'Freudian and other quasi-scientific psychologies are getting away with a concept of truthfulness which belongs essentially to imaginative literature, that in which the opposite of truth is not falsehood but another truth.' In this context the scientific/rational and the literary/mythic approaches to knowledge are profoundly opposed: 'Science tends to expel literature, and literature science from any territory to which they both have claims.'

Imaginative understanding

THERE IS, HOWEVER, another approach to mythology which has tended to fall outside the narrowly scientific thought-collective. In its modern form this is widely attributed to the Italian philosopher, Giambattista Vico (1668–1744), whose outlook has been summarized with admirable clarity by Isaiah Berlin:

> 'Vico looks at myths as evidence of the different categories in which experience was organized – spectacles, unfamiliar to us, through which early man and remote peoples looked at the world in which they lived: the purpose is to understand whence we come, how we came to be where we are, how much or how little of the past we still carry with us. His approach is genetic, for it is only through its genesis, reconstructed by fantasia, guided by rules which he thinks he has discovered, that anything can be truly understood: not by some intuition of timeless essences, or empirical description or analysis of an object's present state.'[46]

And, he continues:

> 'This kind of knowledge is not knowledge of facts or of logical truths, provided by observation or the sciences or deductive reasoning; nor is it knowledge of how to do things; nor the knowledge provided by faith. . . . It is more like the knowledge we claim of a friend, of his character, of his ways of thought or action. . . . To do this, one must possess imaginative power of a high degree, such as artists, and, in particular, novelists require.'

Vico's fantasia, or imaginative understanding, was the forerunner of what was to go by various names – empathy, intuitive sympathy, *Verstehen*, *Einfühlung* – and enable so critical a thinker as Emile Durkheim to put 'mythological truths' alongside 'scientific truths'. In his suggested typology of mythical functions G. S. Kirk distinguishes between the narrative-entertaining, the operative-valedatory, and the speculative-explanatory.[47] Of these it is the explanatory myth, representing an imaginative response to real problems, which is more closely related to scientific thinking. 'The value of myth for science', according to a contemporary assessment:

> 'lies in providing a change of metaphor that creates a fresh focus, a new set of terms for dealing with intellectual material, and thus serves both to explain mental logjams and to provide a source of creativity in the search for answers. Solutions to scientific problems often require metaphors that may not yet be conceptualized.'[48]

Viewed in this perspective, psychoanalysis as myth or 'mythod' can lay claim to scientific consideration, provided, first, that its metaphors are recognized for what they are and, second, that belief in the system as a whole be suspended. For the most part neither condition has been met, so that little headway has been made with its less sympathetic critics. Meanwhile, however, it has become clear that the declining reputation of the system in medical and scientific circles, disciples apart, impinges hardly at all on Freud's 'educated and curious-minded readers' for whom its mass appeal depends precisely on its imaginative rather than on its scientific character. George Steiner, who may be taken as a polymathic representative of these readers, makes no bones about the matter. Conceding that much of classical psychoanalysis has lost any pretence to scientific status and that psychiatrists do not encounter patients who fit the Freudian paradigms, he concludes:

'Freud is one of the great mythologists, one of the great writers and imaginers of an arching metaphor of ordering myth and ritual (the analytic seance). His fantastic overvaluation of the sexual, the archaic alphabet of dreams which he put forward with such stylistic genius, his stoic agnosticism, are fading fast in the sumptuous mausoleum of the central European, middle-class, patriarchal *belle époque*.

No less than Marxism, Freudian psychoanalysis remains one of the feats of the messianic Judaic vision for man after his emancipation from religiosity. Myth, be it that of an Oedipus complex, be it that of an Arcadia of human "adulthood", is of its essence.'[49]

Literature and mythology

A HOST OF imaginative artists have responded gratefully to the metaphors, the language, and the allusions of Freudian theory, whose influence on the visual, literary, and musical arts of the twentieth century has been profound, as the history of the surrealist movement illustrates *par excellence*.[50] Some writers have repaid that debt by an empathic understanding of its source, no one more searchingly than Thomas Mann for whom: 'The mythical interest is as native to psychoanalysis as the psychological interest is to creative writing.'[51] This was, of course, fully recognized by its founder, who expressed his belief on more than one occasion that the roots of neurosis were to be found in mythological sources, and predicted to Carl Jung that together they would conquer the whole field of mythology. The historian of science, Frank Sulloway, concludes his massive study of Freud's thought with a catalogue of the twenty-six major myths which have contributed to the Freud legend.[52] And, significantly, since every narrative myth requires its hero, Sulloway pays special attention not only to the mythic content of Freud's ideas but to the personalization of his role in his own mythology, echoing Jung's perceptive comment of

23

seventy years earlier: 'Like Heracles of old, you are human hero and demi-God, wherefore your dicta unfortunately carry with them a sempiternal value.'[53]

The dicta also carry literary overtones. Thus D. M. Thomas, introducing his remarkable novel *The White Hotel*, speaks explicitly of Freud as 'the discoverer of the great and beautiful myth of psychoanalysis', incorporates him as one of the *dramatis personae*, and includes a wholly convincing clinical case-history, supposedly written by Freud himself, to present his heroine.[54] In justifying the procedure Thomas goes still further, claiming that:

> 'In his case-studies Freud was often fictionalizing. . . . These are white hotel stories that Freud was writing . . . I suspect that for Freud it was just as important to get a good story, a well-shaped classical Greek story, as to get at the truth.'[55]

Recalling Karl Popper's description of *The Interpretation of Dreams* as a collection of Homeric tales, Thomas's comment brings us back to the case-histories, the key-stone of the whole edifice. The few published accounts of Freud's personal cases usually render it difficult, if not impossible, to ascertain their veracity, but there is one exception. Anna Freud has acknowledged that the Wolf Man 'is the only one able and willing to co-operate actively in the reconstruction and follow-up of his case'.[56] Freud's original paper[3] purported to trace the sources of the subject's obsessional symptomatology back to childhood sexual experience, and on these retrospectively prophetic foundations there is constructed an ingenious set of theoretical causes relating to anal eroticism, castration fears, the primal scene, and the psychodynamics of obsessions. At the termination of the four-and-a-half-year long analysis Freud regarded the patient as 'cured'. Some years later, however, he relapsed with a full-blown psychotic disorder, diagnosed by his second psychoanalyst as 'the hypochondriacal type of paranoia',[57] of which no trace had been detected by Freud. Again he was deemed to have been cured, but for the rest of his long life the Wolf Man remained intermittently unwell and dependent on psychiatric support, and in his final years, as alert and introspective as ever, he was persuaded to discuss his life in a series of talks with an independent interviewer. His personal affection for Freud remained undimmed but he was not uncritical of the way in which his doctors had employed Zadig's method, as the following example reveals:

> 'w: In my story, what was explained by dreams? Nothing as far as I can see. Freud traces everything back to the primal scene which he derives from the dream. But that scene does not occur in the dream. When he interprets the white wolves as nightshirts or something like that, for example, linen sheets or clothes, that's somehow far-fetched, I think. That scene in the dream where the windows open and so on and the wolves are sitting there, and his interpretation, I don't know, those things are miles apart. It's terribly far-fetched.
>
> o: But is it true that you did have that dream?
>
> w: Yes it is.

O: You must have told him other dreams.

W: Of course, but I no longer remember the dreams I told him.

O: And that didn't impress you when he interpreted dreams?

W: Well, he said it doesn't matter whether one takes note of that or not, consciously. The effect remains. I think that assertion would have to be proven. I prefer free association because there, something can occur to you. But the primal scene is no more than a construct.

O: You mean the interpretation Freud derives from the dream, that you observed the coitus of your parents, the three acts of coitus?

W: The whole thing is improbable because in Russia, children sleep in the nanny's bedroom, not in their parents'. It's possible, of course, that there was an exception, how do I know? But I have never been able to remember anything of that sort.

In logic, you learn not to go from consequences to cause, but in the opposite direction, from cause to consequences. When, where we have an *a*, we also have a *b*, I must find a *b* when *a* recurs. If one does it the other way around, and concludes from effects to cause, it's the same thing as circumstantial evidence in a trial. But that's a weak argument isn't it? He maintains I saw it, but who will guarantee that it is so? That it is not a fantasy of his? That's one thing. We had best begin with the theory, and, secondly, when one makes something conscious that was in the subconscious, it doesn't help at all. Freud once said, 'I am a spiritual revolutionary''. . . . Well, I also have to look at psychoanalysis critically, I cannot believe everything Freud said, after all. I have always thought that the memory would come. But it never did.'[58]

A striking 'white hotel' story, indeed, and one which may serve as a reminder of how closely this attempt to unravel the Platonic bond between Sherlock Holmes and Sigmund Freud involves the aspects of creative narrative which correspond to the mythic process and whose literary history, as Ricoeur observes, 'is a part of the long tradition emerging from the oral epic tradition of the Greeks, the Celts, and the Germans'.[59] It remains to identify the particular nature of the myth, and in his recently published study of the culture of psychoanalysis the Freudian literary scholar, Professor Steven Marcus, provides a helpful clue:

'A few years before Freud began his great work, another physician-writer made his appearance in London. The work that he began to describe as being conducted at 221B Baker Street, makes for an interesting anticipation of the activities that would shortly begin in the Berggasse. The "methods" of dealing with the material which is brought before the investigator this writer represented are well known. . . . Holmes believes that somehow all these stories actually and eventually make sense, and that he with his special skills can help bring overt and explicit sense to them and therefore to the reality to which they refer and whose structure they elliptically and fragmentarily represent . . . although not everyone can tell it unaided.

25

It is worth noting, however, that the secrets and puzzles and ellipses in these stories always refer to outer reality – to sleeves, thumb-nails, boot-laces, and foot-prints; to wigs and paint and cobbler's wax; to thefts, frauds, lies, plots, and murders. The world is made coherent by solving these external mysteries.

When a few years later in Vienna, the physician-writer-detective with whom we are all familiar began to bring his work to the reading public he would base that work upon a strikingly similar set of assumptions and would present the world with a strikingly similar set of mysterious accounts. What the Viennese Holmes was going to do, however, was to take almost all the mysteries and secrets, and all the incoherent narratives, and place them inside. This shift from outer to inner reality marks a great historical transformation. On the one hand there seems to be something ironic in this circumstance that the detective story as a genre begins to flourish at just about the same moment in history when the locus of the mystery is in the course of dramatic change. On the other hand, the flourishing of the detective story (along with psychoanalysis, one might say) in the modern era does tell us something about the growth of a widespread and popular consciousness that the world has become an increasingly problematical place; that its structure is not immediately apprehensible; that we need help in understanding it; and that there may not be very much about the settled social or psychological order that we can take for granted. One way or another, it appears, we all need a detective. Whether he is a private eye or a third ear, we need him to help us get our lives and their stories straight.'[60]

Detective fiction

WITH THE DETECTIVE story, therefore, we reach the point of our departure after following a trail which has led through cocaine, Zadig's method, the mythopoeic faculty, and imaginative literature. The spectacular success of the detective story as a literary genre over the past 150 years has given rise to several historical studies,[61] and the typology and structure of detective fiction have been analysed with subtlety and erudition by Todorov.[62] In sociological terms it has been argued that 'what crime literature offered to its readers . . . was a reassuring world in which those who tried to disturb the established order were always discovered and published'.[63] Psychological attempts at explanation have included several psychoanalytical interpretations. Thus Rycroft sees the criminal as personifying the reader's unavowed hostility to the parent,[64] while Pederson-Krag has asserted that the origins of the genre are to be found in the primal scene, the murder representing parental intercourse, the reader *qua* detective indulging in infantile curiosity, and Dr Watson supplying 'a safe defence, for should the punishing super-ego threaten, the reader can point to this character and say, "This is I. I was simply standing by." '[65] A more poetic and profound exposition is offered by Auden:

'The fantasy . . . which the detective story addict indulges is the fantasy of being restored to the Garden of Eden, to a state of innocence, where he may know love as love and not as the law. The driving force behind this daydream is a feeling of guilt, the cause of which is unknown to the dreamer. The fantasy of escape is the same, whether one explains the guilt in Christian, Freudian, or any other terms.'[66]

This fertile suggestion has been tellingly extended by Brigid Brophy in her essay on the detective story as secular mythology.[67] In a secularized era which is short of myths, she argues: 'The cause in which the modern detective employs his method and his skills remains the same as that in which the Greek hero uses his magic powers and talismans – the deliverance of the population from a threat.' In detective stories, she continues, 'the only ones which laid down the pattern of a myth, it is guilt which is rationally understood and traced to its source'. On such foundations Sherlock Holmes and Sigmund Freud – the archetypical detective and the prototypical mental healer – are twinned as the contemporary heroes of an ancient legend. They take their place, furthermore, in the wake of the most prophetic myth-maker of the nineteenth century, Friedrich Nietzsche, who anticipated so much of Freud's thinking. It was Nietzsche who proclaimed the quietus of religious belief, equated truth with a new psychology, and predicted the substitution of the old gods by the *Ubermensch*, the new man, detached, quasi-omniscient. When Carl Jung described Nietzsche and Freud as 'answers to the sickness of the nineteenth century', he saw them as Joseph Bell's 'half doctors, half virtuosi'. And much of Holmes's appeal, as Julian Symons observes, is that: 'Far more than any of his later rivals, he was so evidently a Nietzschian superior man.'[63]

Perhaps this is the most fitting note on which to take leave of our two heroes, basking in mutual admiration in the pages of *The Seven Per Cent Solution*, two magi meeting appropriately in the no-man's-land between fact and fiction. The last word should surely go to Dr Watson, moved to bid farewell to his Viennese colleague with the highest compliment in his repertoire: 'Freud, you are the greatest detective of them all.'

References

1   Meyer, N. (1975) *The Seven Per Cent Solution*. London: Hodder & Stoughton.

2   Freud, S. (1918 [1914]) From the History of an Infantile Neurosis. *The Standard Edition of the Complete Psychological Works of Sigmund Freud*, vol. 17. London: The Hogarth Press and the Institute of Psycho-analysis, p. 7.

3   Freud, S. (1943) *Introductory Lectures on Psychoanalysis*. Transl. J. Rivière. (2nd edn). London: George Allen & Unwin.

4   Pankeyev, S. K. (1972) My Recollections of Sigmund Freud. In M. Gardiner (ed.) *The Wolf Man and Sigmund Freud*. London: The Hogarth Press, p. 135.

5   Freud, S. (1974) Letter to C. G. Jung. In W. McGuire (ed.) *The Freud/Jung Letters*. London: The Hogarth Press and Routledge & Kegan Paul, pp. 234–35.

6   Kardiner, A. (1958) Freud – The Man I Knew, the Scientist, and his Influence. In B. Nelson (ed.) *Freud and the Twentieth Century*. London: George Allen & Unwin, p. 46.

7   Occasional Correspondent (1936) Was Sherlock Holmes a Drug Addict? *Lancet* 2: 1,555.

8   Miller, W. H. (1978) The Habit of Sherlock Holmes. *Transactions and Studies of the College of Physicians of Philadelphia*, fifth series, 45:252.

9   Grilly, D. M. (1978) A Reply to Miller's 'The Habit of Sherlock Holmes'. *Transactions and Studies of the College of Physicians of Philadelphia*, fifth series, 45:324.

10 Goodman, L. and Gilman, A. (1975) *The Pharmacological Basis of Therapeutics*. 5th edn. New York: Macmillan, p. 302.

11 Modell, W. (1967) Mass Drug Catastrophes and the Roles of Science and Technology. *Science* 156:346.

12 Doyle, A. C. (1879) Gelsemium as a Poison. *British Medical Journal* 2:483.

13 Jones, E. (1953–57) *Sigmund Freud: Life and Works*. London: The Hogarth Press.

14 Thornton, E. M. (1983) *Freud and Cocaine*. London: Blond & Briggs.

15 Musto, D. F. (1966) Sherlock Holmes and Heredity. *Journal of the American Medical Association* 196(1):45.

16 Astrachan, B. M. and Boltax, S. (1966) The Cyclical Disorder of Sherlock Holmes. *Journal of the American Medical Association* 196(12):142.

17 Vash, G. (1966) The States of Exhaustion of Mr Sherlock Holmes. *Journal of the American Medical Association* 197(8).

18 Musto, D. F. (1968) A Study in Cocaine. *Journal of the American Medical Association* 204(1):27.

19 Klawans, H. L. (1982) The Norwegian Explorer. In *The Medicine of History*. New York: Raven Press, p. 19.

20 How, H. (1892) A Day with Dr Conan Doyle. *Strand Magazine* 4:186.

21 Blathwayt, R. (1892) A Talk with Dr Conan Doyle. *Bookman* 2:50.

22 Doyle, A. C. (1892) Quoted in R. L. Green (ed.) (1983) *The Uncollected Sherlock Holmes*. Harmondsworth: Penguin, p. 18.

23 Saxby, J. M. (1913) *Joseph Bell: An Appreciation by an Old Friend*. Edinburgh: Oliphant, Anderson, & Ferrier.

24 Bell, J. (1892) The Adventures of Sherlock Holmes: A Review. *Bookman* 2:73.

25 Voltaire (1748) Zadig. In *Candide and Other Tales*. Transl. T. Smollett. London: Dent (1937), p. 12.

26 Huxley, T. H. (1881) On the Method of Zadig: Retrospective Prophecy as a Function of Science. In *Science and Culture, and Other Essays*. London: Macmillan (1888), p. 128.

27 Whewell, W. (1847) *The Philosophy of the Inductive Sciences*. London: J. W. Parker.

28 Morelli, G. (1883) *Italian Painters: Critical Studies of the Works*. Transl. L. M. Richter. London: G. Bell & Son.

29 Wollheim, R. (1973) *Giovanni Morelli and the Origins of Scientific Connoisseurship*. In *On Art and the Mind: Essays and Lectures*. London: Allen Lane, p. 177.

30 Castelnuovo, E. (1968) Attribution. In *Encylopaedia Universalis*, vol. II. Paris: Pubs. Encylopaedia Universalis.

31 Wind, E. (1963) *Art and Anarchy*. London: Faber & Faber, p. 32.

32 Ginzburg, C. (1980) Morelli, Freud and Sherlock Holmes: Clues and Scientific Method. *History Workshop* 9:5.

33 Freud, S. (1914) The Moses of Michelangelo. *The Standard Edition of the Complete Psychological Works of Sigmund Freud*, vol. 13. London: The Hogarth Press and the Institute of Psycho-analysis, p. 222. Originally published in *Imago* 3(1):15–36.

34 Hauser, A. (1959) *The Philosophy of Art History*. London: Routledge & Kegan Paul.

35 Wilson, J. A. C. (1984) 'Greatly Exaggerated.' Letter to *The Times*, 19 July.

36 Auden, W. H. (1975) Dingley Dell and the Fleet. In *The Dyer's Hand and Other Essays*. London: Faber & Faber, p. 407.

37 Kittle, C. F. (1981) Sir Arthur Conan Doyle – Physician and Detective. Proceedings of the Institute of Medicine, Chicago 34:7.

38 Isherwood, C. (1969) 'The Speckled Band' by Arthur Conan Doyle. In *Exhumations*. Harmondsworth: Penguin, p. 106.

39 Pearsall, R. (1977) *Conan Doyle: A Biographical Solution*. London: Weidenfeld & Nicolson.

40 Freud, S. (1953) The Interpretation of Dreams. Transl. J. Strachey. *The Standard Edition of the Complete Psychological Works of Sigmund Freud*, vols 4 and 5. London: The Hogarth Press and the Institute of Psycho-analysis.

41 Strachey, J. (1962) Sigmund Freud: A Sketch of His Life and Ideas. In *Two Short Accounts of Psychoanalysis*. Harmondsworth: Pelican.

42 Conn, J. H. (1974) The Decline of Psychoanalysis. *Journal of the American Medical Association* 228(6):711.

43 Medawar, P. B. (1972) Further Comments on Psychoanalysis. In *The Hope of Progress*. London: Methuen, p. 57.

44 Fisher, S. and Greenberg, R. P. (1977) *The Scientific Credibility of Freud's Theories and Therapy*. Brighton: Harvester Press.

45 Medawar, P. B. (1969) Science and Literature. *Encounter* 32(1):15.

46 Berlin, I. (1981) The Divorce between the Sciences and the Humanities. In *Against the Current*. London: Oxford University Press.

47 Kirk, G. S. (1970) *Myth: Its Meaning and Function in Ancient and Other Cultures*. Cambridge: Cambridge University Press.

48 O'Flaherty, W. D. (1980) Inside and Outside the Mouth of God: the Boundary between Myth and Reality. *Daedalus* Spring: 93.

49 Steiner, G. (1984) Review of J. M. Masson's *Freud: The Assault on Truth*. *The Sunday Times* 27 May.

50 Nadeau, M. (1964) *Histoire du Surréalisme*. Paris: Éditions du Seuil.

51 Mann, T. (1937) Freud and the Future. In *Essays of Three Decades*. New York: Knopf.

52 Sulloway, F. (1979) *Freud, Biologist of the Mind*. London: Burnett Books.

53 Jung, C. G. (1974) Letter to Freud, 14.12.09. In W. McGuire (ed.) *The Freud/Jung Letters*. London: The Hogarth Press and Routledge & Kegan Paul, p. 275.

54 Thomas, D. M. (1981) *The White Hotel*. London: Gollancz.

55 Thomas, D. M. (1983) Freud and the 'White Hotel'. *British Medical Journal* 287(ii):1,957.

56 Freud, A. (1972) Foreword to M. Gardiner (ed.) *The Wolf Man and Sigmund Freud*. London: The Hogarth Press and the Institute of Psycho-analysis, p. IX.

57 Brunswick, R. M. (1928) A Supplement to Freud's 'History of an Infantile Neurosis'. *The International Journal of Psychoanalysis* 9:439.

58 Obholzer, K. (1982) *The Wolf Man Sixty Years Later*. London: Routledge & Kegan Paul.

59 Ricoeur, P. (1977) The Question of Proof in Freud's Psychoanalytic Writings. *Journal of the American Psychoanalytic Association* 25:835.

60 Marcus, S. (1984) *Freud and the Culture of Psychoanalysis*. London: George Allen & Unwin.

61 Barzun, J. (1971) *A Catalogue of Crime*. New York: Harper & Row.

62 Todorov, T. (1977) The Typology of Detective Fiction. In *The Poetics of Prose*. Transl. R. Howard. Oxford: Blackwell, p. 42.

63 Symons, J. (1972) *Bloody Murder*. London: Faber & Faber.

64 Rycroft, C. (1957) A Detective-story. *The Psychoanalytic Quarterly* 26:229.

REFERENCES

65 Pederson-Krag, G. (1949) Detective Stories and the Primal Scene. *The Psychoanalytic Quarterly* **18**:207.

66 Auden, W. H. (1963) The Guilty Vicarage. In *The Dyer's Hand and Other Essays.* London: Faber & Faber, p. 146.

67 Brophy, B. (1966) Detective Fiction: A Modern Myth of Violence. In *Don't Never Forget.* London: Cape, p. 121.